The Catholic Playbook

Lenten Reflections for Single Catholics

FOREWORD BY BISHOP KEVIN RHOADES

Edited by Christina Ries
CatholicMatch Editorial Director

Prayers by Father Gary C. Caster

Cover Design: Elisco Advertising

Interior design: Creative Editorial Solutions

ISBN: 978-0-9849604-0-8

Printed in the United States of America

Table of Contents

Preface

"A Yearly Checkpoint"

When we began reflecting on Lent and single life, the parallels fascinated us. Both are seasons of solitude and sacrifice, periods that invite us to draw closer to God. Both are set-aside stages to take up our crosses, guided by the promise of the risen Lord.

Single life, like the Lenten journey, is not for the fainthearted. We're talking about uphill battles. But we know every turn brings new graces, so we press onward – heads up, hearts open.

We wanted to explore these parallels more deeply, and to do that, we knew we needed to go directly to the source, so we asked single Catholics to reflect on the two seasons. We were amazed by what poured forth, reflections that are sure to both challenge and comfort you. They are earnest and honest, spelling out every doubt and fear while revealing an underlying faith. Some contemplate the pain of divorce or the death of a spouse. Others are written by Catholics who have never married and are seeking a mate. Still others come from singles who are considering religious life.

One single told us that Lent is a "yearly checkpoint," and you'll see that these writers are taking stock, reflecting back and looking forward. They are counting the days of Lent and their birthdays, spotting mile markers, gauging the singles scene, sizing up the situation. This book contains self assessment of the highest order. The twin results: self discipline and self discovery.

Each reflection concludes with a prayer written by the wonderful Father Gary Caster, a college chaplain who contributes to EWTN and *Magnificat*. We hope you'll sit and pray with his words, letting them sink into your heart. Our favorite passage comes from Day 29, when Father Caster writes: "Teach me your desert wisdom so that I can move through these 40 days more closely united to You and Your Father's will."

We love the phrase "desert wisdom." It is, indeed, what we seek each Lent: words to live by, guideposts for a scorched journey. We hope and pray you find exactly that in these pages.

Read on!

– The CatholicMatch Staff

Foreword

"The Divine Thirst"

The Savior hangs before you with a pierced heart.
He has spilled His heart's blood to win your heart.

These beautiful words by St. Teresa Benedicta of the Cross, known to the world as Edith Stein, speak of the love of Christ the bridegroom for His beloved bride. Throughout the long centuries of salvation history, the image that the authors of sacred Scripture, inspired by the Holy Spirit, used most frequently to describe the love God has for His people was that of a husband for his wife. When the fullness of time had come, He became like us in all things but sin, living with us, and even more deeply, for us, until the final consummation of His love on Calvary.

As Bl. John Paul II reflected: "The 'sincere gift' contained in the sacrifice of the Cross gives definitive prominence to the spousal meaning of God's love. As the Redeemer of the world, Christ is the Bridegroom of the Church... In the context of the 'great mystery' of Christ and of the Church, all are called to respond – as a bride – with the gift of their lives to the inexpressible gift of the love of Christ" (Mulieris Dignitatem, 26-27). On the cross Christ made a complete gift of Himself, not only to the Church as a whole, but to each of us personally, and He wants nothing more – and nothing less – than our complete gift of self in return. Christ longs for a deep, intimate, personal relationship with each of us, in which we entrust everything – our dreams, our desires, our sufferings, our will – to His loving embrace.

Lent is the holy season when we contemplate in a deeper way the tremendous love which the Lord has for each of us and we recommit ourselves to respond to that love with the gift of our lives. The reflections in this book have been written by single Catholics who are striving to love the Lord more deeply during these 40 days. Like the psalms, they are written from the heart and express the full range of human emotions: longing and loneliness, repentance and purification, periods of intense suffering and moments of deep joy. They bear poignant witness to the fact that whatever is in our hearts can be offered to Christ as part of our complete gift of self to Him. As the Catechism of the Catholic Church points out, when we pray we need to come before the Lord as we are, in all humility and honesty: "We let our masks fall and turn our hearts back to the Lord who loves us, so as to hand ourselves over to Him as an offering to be purified and transformed" (CCC #2711).

This Lent, I encourage you who are single to focus on the stunning fact that the yearning you feel in your heart to find a human spouse is precisely the yearning which the Lord feels for you. When He said, "I thirst" from the cross, He was thirsting for your love. Prayer, the *Catechism* teaches, is the intimate moment when his thirst meets ours, as the Samaritan woman discovered at the well of Sychar: "The wonder of prayer is revealed beside the well where we come seeking water: There, Christ comes to meet every human being. It is He who first seeks us and asks us for a drink. Jesus thirsts; His asking arises from the depths of God's desire for us. Whether we realize it or not, prayer is the encounter of God's thirst with ours. God thirsts that we might thirst for Him...Prayer is a response of love to the thirst of the only Son of God" (CCC #2560-2561).

It is my hope that the reflections which follow will be springboards for your own prayer as you deepen your relationship with the Lord during these 40 days. You will come to discover that intimate union with Him is the pearl of great price which alone satisfies the deepest desires of the human heart. And you will know the peace that only He can give, a peace which St. Teresa Benedicta of the Cross sensed as she began to realize that what she had planned for herself paled in comparison with what the Bridegroom had planned for her:

"Things were in God's plan which I had not planned at all. I am coming to the living faith and conviction that – from God's point of view – there is no chance and that the whole of my life, down to every detail, has been mapped out in God's divine providence and makes complete and perfect sense in God's all-seeing eyes."

The Savior of the world wants to be your Spouse. Won't you let Him win your heart this Lent?

– Bishop Kevin Rhoades

A User's Guide

When the Catholic Church counts 40 days of Lent, it excludes Sundays. That's because every Sunday is considered a celebration of Jesus' resurrection on Easter Sunday and, hence, a break from the disciplines of Lent. So when you use this book, remember to skip Sundays. The 40 days of Lent begin with Ash Wednesday and end with Holy Saturday, on the eve of Easter.

Day One

"I Recognize How Much I Need God's Grace"

Lent has begun! Soon I'll be hearing tales of what my Catholic friends and acquaintances have given up. This practice can become a cliché, devoid of any real meaning if not done without careful consideration.

As part of my Lenten practice, I do give something up, but it must be something I'll be longing for with every part of me. When I have chosen the right sacrifice, these 40 days of Lent can seem like an eternity.

Perhaps that's why the single life can often feel like Lent: I feel that something is missing, something I truly desire and yearn for. I find myself waiting and hoping for a long period of time to come to an end.

While singleness is partly choice, it is also part circumstance, not having been able to find the right person.

Unlike my Lenten sacrifice, which can easily be broken, the single life is not so easy to break if I want to experience what I am really looking for. The 40 days of Lent, like life, cannot be rushed if we are to truly appreciate and rejoice in a glorious Easter.

I am reminded of the antiphon for mid-afternoon prayer during Lent in the Liturgy of the Hours: "Armed with God's justice and power, let us prove ourselves through patient endurance."

This is where my Lenten sacrifice and single life intertwine. For both, I recognize how much I need God's grace – the former to give me the strength to patiently endure in the face of temptation, the latter to patiently endure until the right time and person come along.

Because the single life is indefinite, perhaps it's time to look to Lent as a way to let God strengthen us in patient endurance.

—————⬥—————

Father, the season of Lent opens a way for us to see our lives are intertwined with the life of Your Son. When the desires of my heart prevent me from seeing Your justice and power at work within the ordinary circumstances of my life, fill me with greater patience so that I may endure the time between that for which I long and the unfolding of Your plan.

Day Two

"We Have to Read Between the Lines"

Last Sunday I became a grandmother for the second time. Yippee!

My son and his wife had a beautiful baby girl whom they named Grace Elizabeth. The name fits her perfectly since she was born when I was at Sunday Mass.

All week I have been reflecting on what a true blessing Gracie is for our family and how easy it is to love her.

This stands in stark contrast to the emotions I felt when my first granddaughter, Madeline Jean, was born. You see, my husband and oldest son had passed away not too long before Maddie's birth. I was stuck in a dark, lonely place when she arrived. Happiness seemed difficult to bear.

The joy of her birth was choked by the anguish I felt at going alone to the hospital. Fortunately, my youngest brother volunteered to go with me. While I held the baby, he stood quietly in the corner of the hospital room, offering the gentle moral support of a kid brother. As long as I live I will never forget this kindness.

With the birth of Grace, it seems I have come full circle. I delight in being a grandmother and spoiling these sweet little girls. It's so much fun since we raised three sons. Now I'm relishing the pink daintiness, the bows and ruffles and giggles. To me, there's a clear lesson: God is good all the time – we just have to read between the lines.

The heartache I suffered after the deaths of my son and husband seem similar, but small in comparison, to the suffering Jesus endured on the cross. Much as His rising from the dead on Easter Sunday brings back the Alleluia in our lives, so in His great mercy has He put the Alleluia back in my life with Maddie and Gracie.

<hr />

Lord Jesus, Your time in the desert and Your way to the Cross teach me that You understand what it's like to be in dry and lonely places. Help me trust the Father as You did, securing my hope in His goodness. Teach me to read between the lines of my pain and sorrow in order to discover the delight You take in me. Put on my lips the Alleluia that You sung both on the way to the cross and when You rose triumphant from the grave.

Day Three

"I Think of This as Preparation Time"

My appreciation for Lent has deepened in recent years, and I've been able to use this season to strengthen my relationship with Christ.

Although romantic relationships can be fun and exciting, I've come to realize they can also be a distraction. Being single has allowed me to focus on my relationship with Christ and to have a closer encounter with Him.

During Lent I attend holy hour and the Stations of the Cross on Fridays nights. Spending this time in reflection has helped me tremendously, not only in my spiritual life but also to begin to see the woman God intended me to be. I like to think of this as a preparation time, a time to prepare for a healthy relationship in the future.

I've also found that this is a great time of year to evangelize our Catholic faith, our traditions, and why we do what we do. Unfortunately, I have some friends – both Catholic and non-Catholic – who have a hard time understanding why I spend my Friday nights at church during Lent. Sometimes they tease that I should be a nun.

I know I'm part of the minority in my age group, but I don't let that bother me. I feel blessed to have a relationship with God and a desire to grow in my faith. This is the one true relationship that will last forever. The more you invest in this relationship, the better off you'll be. Lent is the perfect time to improve it.

As for finding my future spouse, I have decided to leave my request to the One who knows best.

⇒◆⇐

Good and gracious God, Your Son teaches us that our lives here and now are a preparation for our lives with You forever. Help me surrender whatever I desire that is not in accordance with Your plan. You alone know that which is best for me, so by Your grace, shape my life into a wordless proclamation of Your saving love.

Day Four

"God Loves a Good Comeback"

Long distances come into play with any dating site. She lives on the other side of the country, yet his heart burns for her. How can it be, Lord, that you allow two people meant for each other to be separated by such long distances?

I turn to the book of Tobit for light. Tobit sends his son Tobias to Rages to collect a large sum of money. The Archangel Raphael guides and accompanies Tobias on the long journey because Tobias doesn't know the way. Raphael leads him on a side trip to Ecbatana, where Tobias finds his future wife, Sarah.

All of us are walking with St. Raphael on this road to where that special someone is waiting – the many single Jacobs and Sarahs out there.

Walking this road is a Lent in itself, a Lent of waiting,

anticipating and fasting for how God will answer our desires at the end of the journey.

No one is alone in this walk of faith. The devil might throw the kitchen sink at you, as he did Sarah, wiping out her first seven husbands, yet one got through – the one accompanied by St. Raphael!

Continue with St. Raphael, who will heal you along the way as he creams the devil in the process!

We can't always fix the damage from our past relationships or the pain from rejections, but God loves a good comeback, and as in the example of Sarah, who was against the ropes and ready for the towel; it was then that her simple prayer was heard.

As you travel on this mysterious road to your beloved this Lent, know that Jesus, our true Beloved, is at the end of that road too, waiting with open arms.

—————

Lord, You alone are the "someone special" for whom all hearts long. As we continue on the road that leads to You, keep us ever mindful that we are never alone. Your holy angels accompany us on our way, serving our needs and safeguarding our lives. Let me be for others what Your angels are for me and make my life an embodied sign for others that they are never alone or separated from You.

Day Five

"I Felt Stuck in a Second Adolescence"

This Lent I would finally like to follow the pope's suggestion that we fast from our dependence on technology. I am taking a 40-day fast from a particular social networking site, which I suspect I've become slightly addicted to.

I knew I was spending a lot of time on the site, but I realized the issues went deeper than wasted time. I became uncomfortable when my friends and I would collectively trash a musician, mock some fallen celebrity or engage in negative political discourses.

In the words of one of my favorite Jesuits, Father James Martin, I feel I've become one of the people who forgot "Jesus' words in our digital age, when snarky blogs, terrible texting, snotty Facebook posts and mean-spirited tweets zip around the Web and cause serious harm."

This perfectly encapsulates the discomfort I felt. I tended to think of celebrity-trashing as a victimless crime, because obviously famous people aren't reading my posts. But it's a matter of being charitable and empathic in speech, no matter who is being discussed.

My quasi-addiction to social networking also revealed another issue: It served as a painful reminder that I had time to waste because I had no spouse or children to attend to. In a sense I felt stuck in a second adolescence, having time to hang out online with no responsibilities.

But I'd often had a distant, nagging feeling that I should be doing something more useful. Of course that feeling usually faded the minute a friend logged on to chat or posted a video clip that interested me. And while the teenager within me was satisfied, the adult remained unproductive…and unmarried.

Knowing that the Lenten season is a threefold attempt to remind us of Christian ethics, I also plan on adding to my prayer life and to works of charity. So I'm going back to the practice of Centering Prayer.

Finally, I plan on visiting Potter's Field, a cemetery for homeless New Yorkers. I'm going with a non-denominational charity which gathers bi-monthly to pray before the unmarked graves for all the souls of the forgotten.

"I Felt Stuck in a Second Adolescence"

Almighty and ever living God, we do well always to center ourselves in You. Help me to be strong in securing my identity in the truth of self revealed by Your Son, Jesus Christ. Through the gift of Your Holy Spirit, do not allow my feelings to cloud my judgment of You, myself, others, or of the world. Let me be wholly dependent upon you and you alone.

Day Six

"No One Said This Was Going to Be Easy"

I was beginning to feel positively medieval.

I had just mentioned to a woman I was dating that premarital sex was out.

"What?" she replied. "In this day and age?"

That was to be expected, I suppose. What was unexpected was that my Lenten mortifications would evoke the same response from her.

Now, I'm no candidate for the monastery. I'm a revert, and I admit that I tend to make up for lost time and go a little further in my faith than is fashionable.

But I had no idea that a resolution to fast all through Lent was going to cause such concern. Limiting myself to lunch at noon, coffee in the morning, and a collation in the evening didn't seem extreme to me, but it did to a woman I was interested in. (The funny thing was that she was always watching what she ate very closely to maintain her admittedly exquisite figure.) Perhaps my eating modifications done for God seemed a little crazy.

But that's the way it is these days. Self-denial in the age of living-for-the-moment is not always attractive. It may even smack of self-abuse.

No one said this was going to be easy. I remember the moment I decided to come back to the Church and to bring the woman I was dating at the time with me. That time the reply was, "Couldn't Catholicism just be your thing and I can have my own thing?"

I'm sure it seemed reasonable, but I knew it was a recipe for disaster. She was an excellent cook, and at the very least, I knew that would mean running a gauntlet of temptations during every Lent. When a beautiful woman cooks you dinner, you're a goner – I don't care how holy you are.

Heavenly Father, the only food that truly sustains us is the meal You provide in the Body and Blood of Your Son. Every time I enjoy a meal or sit and dine, let me be mindful of the altar table You have set before us and of the banquet feast of the Lamb in heaven. Let my Lenten fasting make me hungry for that which is Yours, and instill within me distaste for anything that would encourage me to take the easy way out and satiate my heart with gratitude for all that You have given me.

Day Seven

"Waiting for Our Lives to Begin"

Because we're single, most people assume our lives are fun, ambitious, and rather self-centered. I can attest that that is not true for many of us, who can rarely find a minute to breathe.

Living the single life is a daily challenge, even for those of us embracing it. Lent is a penitential time of prayerful sacrifice, giving, and fasting. As I explained this wonderful liturgical season to my junior-high religious education class, I began to recognize what an impact it can have on our lives, no matter what our age.

Prayerful sacrifice as a single person can be difficult because often we feel as if we're waiting for our lives to begin, so what can I sacrifice?

What about our egos? The Litany of Humility is one of

the simplest but most difficult prayers I have ever uttered. It asks us to set aside our wants and pray that others receive the blessings we desire.

One of our priests recently gave his homily on forgiveness, which is what Lent is all about. The first step to find peace through forgiveness is to identify with whom you need to find peace. Make a list of those people. Then identify all your personal prayer intentions and, finally, pray for those listed people, that they may receive all that you want for yourself.

Now, that's a challenging approach, but when I explain to my students all that Jesus humbled Himself to do for us, this task seems miniscule in comparison.

So take a moment this Lent to release yourself of your desire – whether it's for a partner, a friend, or just a greater sense of community – and humbly pray that others receive it. If we all pray for each other without regard for our own wants, then miracles will happen.

―――⇒∙◇∙⇐―――

Lord Jesus, Your time among us was a time of miracles, but not one of them can compare with the miracle of the forgiveness of our sins. Life really began for us when You emptied Yourself of every desire except that of confirming for us the Father's love. Help me never lose sight of this truth, no matter my age or the daily challenges of life. Let everything I do be a reflection of Your efficacious love so that others may be drawn into an intimate and lasting encounter with You.

Day Eight

"I'm Worried I Have Drifted Off Course"

I've always loved the wind.

You can't help but notice nature. The trees bend in homage. The leaves compete to see who can hold on the longest. Snowflakes shimmy and twirl.

On the Kansas plains, I remember watching the wind blow in a line of clouds, so of course, I also love storms.

Perhaps it is only natural that one of my favorite Gospel stories is that of Jesus calming the storms. Jesus could be found in the storms. That's where some of us recognize Him most easily.

If I had been in that boat, I know I would have been one of the first to recognize Him because I would have been out looking at the sea and enjoying the storm. I would have been jumping up and down in excitement and pointing,

"Look, He's coming!"

This Lent I am asking myself: "What about the boat that I am in today? Would I recognize Jesus today?"

I'm worried that I may have drifted a little off course. It is calm, but my boat is empty. There is no one else here. There don't appear to be any safe harbors. I am isolated and drifting. There is no wind. My sails are limp.

It just feels as though I am moving too slowly – drifting further out into the deep, away from everyone else. And so I pray:

Dear God, don't let me get lost. Please send someone to help me navigate. It would make the journey so much more pleasant. Together, we could count the stars and marvel at your wonderful creation as we watch a sunset. But if that's not possible, please just send me a little wind. Fill my sails and help me soar closer and closer to my final destination. Amen.

—————⟫◆⟪—————

Father, Your Son's life shows us that we are always moving toward the safe harbor of Your love. Let the wind of Your Holy Spirit fill my heart and lift my spirits so that I might continue ever onward in fulfillment of Your plan for me. Make me increasingly aware of Your presence, especially in the calm, still, empty moments of my pilgrim journey.

Day Nine

"I'm Happy to Take a Break from Dating"

I haven't been in many dating relationships, but when I have been in a relationship, it was always a struggle to balance time with my friends and time with my girlfriend.

True, this time does not have to be mutually exclusive, but we all know iron sharpens iron and watching a game while eating greasy pizza hardly qualifies as a romantic date.

This Lent I am excited to be single! While I am not going to go so far as to swear off women altogether, I am definitely not actively searching.

Being single gives me the opportunity to spend date night in prayer, donate the money that would have funded a nice dinner to the Rice Bowl, and spend Saturday volunteering or helping community members with their spring-cleaning projects.

I am going to take this Lent and in a way date Jesus: Spent extra time in prayer with Him, share my gifts with Him, and spend my extra money on Him.

I know that when I take the time in a dating relationship to do these things, they pay off 10-fold. I also know that when I take the time to do these things in my relationship with God, they pay off 10,000-fold.

So don't get me wrong: I don't want to spend the rest of my Lents being single. I am truly looking forward to the day my wife and I can draw closer to the Lord and to each other during Lent by praying and serving together.

However, that day will not be this Lent, and I'm happy to take a break from dating women to have some good ol' quality guy time with Jesus.

⸺◆⸺

Lord Jesus, often You would step away from your disciples to be alone with the Father in prayer. Help me to recognize the times in my life when it would be good for me to be alone with You. May the season of Lent be just such a time. Through the care and attentiveness I bring to the disciplines of Lent, deepen my prayer, strengthen my heart, and refresh my willingness to serve.

Day Ten

"God Might Be Trying to Teach Us Something Vital"

When I saw my boyfriend's profile on a free dating site last March, I figured he had given me up for Lent. When Easter came and I saw him pictured with another woman on Facebook, I knew he had given me up forever.

Nevertheless, I slid on my sparkling jacket, wore my shimmery beads, and wrote "Happy Mardi Gras!" on my classroom whiteboard as the time for Lent drew nigh. With my Catholic family around the world, Ash Wednesday found me fasting and at Mass in preparation for the resurrection of our Savior. I offer yet a different sacrifice this year.

Since my conversion to Catholicism, things given up have included bread, chocolate, sweets, even credit cards. Things added have ranged from reading my Bible to picking up trash to listing 10 blessings daily.

The most difficult sacrifice, however, was two years ago when I vowed to give away a dollar each day of Lent. Unilaterally, I decided that the money had to go to someone in need, such as a student without lunch money or a homeless person at an intersection.

Sadly, by Good Friday I had distributed only one dollar and ended up giving the leftover $39 to the Church, greatly disappointed that the money had not served to make me feel generous or altruistic, nor had it even prodded me to approach the people I was specifically targeting.

Maybe it's like that when we attempt romantic relationships too. While we singles have our own intentions and expectations as we journey, God might be trying to teach us something more vital so we may become better Christians. Whether we are adding or deducting, discovering or dating, let us always keep asking how each experience brings us closer to the Creator.

———◆———

Creator of the universe, generously You chose to make man and woman in Your image and likeness, thereby creating us for love. Sustain me in Your love and help me recognize whatever in my life hinders me from acknowledging Your blessings and prevents me from drawing closer to You. Teach me how to let go of my expectations, however noble they may, so that in every moment and all circumstances I will wholeheartedly say, "Thy will be done."

Day Eleven

"Remember, We Are Purifying Our Love"

The holy season of Lent calls us to purify our love.

Personally, I approach Lent with trepidation: *Am I ready to enter more deeply into myself? Am I ready to acknowledge my sins and do penance? Am I ready for sacrifice?*

In the face of all these questions, I am reminded of one simple fact: Love always requires sacrifice. The lover is willing to die for the sake of the beloved. Christ is the greatest lover in the history of creation. We, as his humble disciples, are called to be like our Divine Master.

In our anticipation of the joys and rewards we may find in a future spouse, we often overlook our own need for preparation to the awesome responsibility of marriage.

For the sake of my spouse, God will require a pure and heroic love free from self-interest, self-gratification, and pride. The holy mother Church thus offers us this beautifully difficult time of purification and, in it, we can embrace the daily deaths that will serve to purify our love for the great demands of His holy will.

Each penance we offer to God teaches us something about the true meaning of love and each sacrifice we make out of love of God will also purify our love for our neighbor for the sake of God. We will have no neighbor more cherished than our future spouse.

As we slog through this season of penance, it is good to remember we are purifying our love – foremost for God, our one true love, but also for the good of our future spouse.

The happiness we will find in the future will be all the more poignant as it is strengthened by a pure love. That is the gift of Lent: It allows us to prepare for the task set before us, the glorious and fearful call to love.

———————

Lord Jesus, throughout these 40 days of Lent the Church offers us a short but intensive course on love. Let the disciplines of Lent be a welcome gift of purification and a joyful experience of penance and sacrifice. Through my willing embrace of my Lenten practices, let me learn the lessons of Your own sacrificial loving so that I might better accept the sacrificial loving to which You call all of Your followers.

Day Twelve

"In the Quiet I Can Hear God's Voice"

My pastor, a Redemptorist, proclaimed in his homily last Sunday that Lent is a time for prayer, almsgiving, and asking forgiveness for sins. This is the time of year when I am really aware of my shortcomings, so I go to reconciliation. It cleanses my soul, and afterwards I always feel light and carefree.

I pray for God's will in my life each day, that He will lead me to make the right decisions in all matters, big and small. I've made a promise this Lent to read about one saint a day to inspire me to become more like Jesus.

Being a single parent, I find great comfort in knowing there were saints such as St. Elizabeth Ann Seton and St. Elizabeth of Hungary who were also single parents striving to lead a holy life.

I'm increasing the amount of time I spend reading Scripture and meditating on His sacred word. I find the best time to read His holy word and pray is in the morning, before my son wakes up. In the quiet and stillness, I can hear His voice more clearly, and it sets my mood in the right direction for the day.

I'm trying to be more prepared when I come across a homeless person; I can give him a ready-made tuna kit. I can also bring food donations to St. Vincent de Paul to feed the poor and clothes my son has outgrown to the domestic abuse shelter.

Although I pray with my son before every meal and before he goes to bed, I'm setting aside a special time for evening prayer together before piano or choir practice. When Easter arrives and we celebrate our Lord's resurrection, I'll have a deeper appreciation for his loving sacrifice.

———◆———

Almighty God, the lives of the saints remind me in a special way that I need Your help each day, in every situation I face and in each decision I make, whether large or small. Their lives also teach me the importance of Your sacred word, not merely for instruction, but as a sure and certain way of transforming my thoughts and stirring my imagination. Let what I learn this Lent become a way of life for me.

Day Thirteen

"I Always Find Excuses"

Being single (and without a roommate), I tend to have a lot of time to reflect once I go home for the evening.

I think about a lot of things, but lately my thoughts seem to revolve around finding someone special to put into my life. I don't intend to stay single forever, so a decent portion of my evening goes towards trying to meet new people and making new friendships.

Lent is also a time of reflection, but to me it's different from my regular reflection; it is a time to reflect on other things I should be working on. The Church challenges us to find something in our lives that would take us out of our comfort zone. For me it is changing something I know I should change but never do because I always find excuses, reasons that the time isn't right.

Reading the Bible has been on my to-do list for quite some time. I know I don't need to read it in one sitting or even over the course of several months. But for whatever reason, I can't even seem to find 15-30 minutes a few times a week to read it.

The current excuse is that I'm trying to find that special person and that the time reading would be better spent searching.

This Lenten season that cycle has changed. I'm making it a priority to read the Bible a few nights a week. I need to have faith that God will continue to help me in my search, even as I partake in other activities.

———◆———

Lord, we know that all times and seasons are of Your making, and yet often in our haste to satisfy our hearts, we try to make them our own. Even when we have the best intentions we need to be reminded that the comfort we seek and the companionship we desire can only truly be satisfied by You. Let the story of Your love in sacred Scripture guide me throughout these 40 days and beyond them, through all the seasons of my life.

Day Fourteen

"I Want to Have Faith Like a Child"

I turn 40 this Lent. I can't say I am dreading this birthday or eagerly anticipating it. A part of me is a little heartbroken I am crossing over one of the last vestiges of youth. In my head, I am still a young girl. I don't feel like I'm 40, but then, what does 40 feel like?

In Biblical terms it is a "very long time." A long time in the desert. A long time of rain and flood. A long time of facing temptation and hunger. A long time of prayer and solitude.

I'm walking through this Lent as I've walked through most of them: alone. While I am surrounded by friends and family, I see the Lenten journey as one that I take myself.

Of course, Jesus is my companion with whom I seek out some heart-to-hearts – His Sacred Heart to my somewhat stony one.

Forty years does a number on a heart. I am recommitting myself to pursuing heart health – physically, emotionally, and spiritually. Living alone means being life coach, motivator, punisher, and consoler all rolled into one.

I've been a CatholicMatch member for seven years, a "very long time." My stony heart – one that has become a little jaded, cynical, broken, impatient, and doubtful – needs to soften and open.

I want to again have faith like a child. I want to believe again wholeheartedly that love and my dreams are within grasp. Putting my piglet heart (as I call it) in the Sacred Heart of Jesus is the best medicine. It doesn't guarantee that my heart won't get hurt. In fact, it is a sure path to the pain of the cross. But it does mean that my heart will beat with a divine love.

Create in me a clean heart, O Lord.

———◆———

Loving Father, through the prophets You taught us to hope for redemption, for the time when You would take our stony hearts and give us fleshy ones in their place. Father, through the sometimes long, drawn out hours of these 40 days, "create a clean heart in me." Rejuvenate that heart given to me through the waters of baptism and the power of the Holy Spirit. Let me be once more and forever Your child – patient and kind, humble and peaceful, joyful and unafraid.

Day Fifteen

"Lent Is Not a Dark and Gloomy Time"

Sacrifice can't happen without love. It is a voluntary act beyond what is required; anything less than love is merely payment for services rendered.

When dating, I start with sacrifice. I get rid of distractions that prevent me from giving my girlfriend my full attention. I look for ways to make her smile. I seek to keep myself pure for her, inside and out, appearing at my best at all times and putting her above my own needs.

It is sacrifice, but because it's out of love, it's never hardship.

It's often said that strong faith will help us find the one we will spend the rest of our lives with, but it's more likely to work in the opposite direction. The strongest force behind my growth in faith over the years has been from the women whom I have loved, teaching me what love truly means.

There is a reason why God uses marriage to describe his relationship with us. Because of this, Lent is not a dark and gloomy time any more than your own preparations for a date could be. It is a time of affection and celebration, preparing to bring the One who is true love more fully into your life. Preparation like that, when done out of love, can never be hardship.

So take the time to prepare for the Lord. Wash yourself, paying attention to those little blemishes that might make you look less than your best. Put on your finest and avoid seeming gloomy or stressed.

Easter will be a date to remember…and who knows? It might just lead to a long and happy relationship.

——⇒·◇·⇐——

Good and gracious God, You have given us this joyful season in order to prepare ourselves to celebrate the Paschal Mystery and the way Your Son purchased our redemption. Help me to use this time wisely, taking advantage of everything the Church offers and all that she recommends. On Easter Sunday may Your Son see me at my best, my heart eager to receive Him and ready to be renewed by the gift of His true love.

Day Sixteen

"My God, Why Have You Forsaken Me?"

Jesus, these 40 days are difficult. I want to walk the road to Calvary with You, but I know the road is long.

I have seen long roads before, times when I didn't know the way, times when the path seemed too steep to climb. I am afraid of the twists and turns, and I am afraid of losing sight of You.

Help me to remember how, on the way to the cross, Your mother was there. Help me to remember to turn to her, for she is familiar with sorrow. She is there to wipe away tears and to bring me back to You.

On the night before You died, You asked Your followers to keep watch for one hour. In the busy grind of daily life, I too become distracted, forgetting You are there, waiting for me. There are times my focus drifts to my sometimes frustrating search for a spouse. I forget about the people around me who need my help.

Help me to remember You are right there with me, closer than any human companion. Help me to listen for Your still, small voice so I may see the needs of the people along the path.

On the cross You felt abandoned, crying out to the Heavenly Father, "My God, My God, why have you forsaken me?" How often have I asked that same question, not when my life was in danger, but when it hasn't turned out quite the way I imagined it should? I am familiar with that prayer.

Help me, Jesus, to keep this time of loneliness in perspective, and when I am feeling abandoned, help me to turn to You, for You know what it feels like to be alone.

———◆———

Jesus, at the foot of the Cross You entrusted Your mother to us through the Apostle John so that she could accompany us along the pathways of our lives. Whenever I lose sight of You or find myself worn out by the twists and turns that distract me from seeing clearly the way marked out for me, help me to hear her gentle and loving voice calling me back to You, ensuring me that I am never alone and that Father never abandons any of his children, especially when they feel frightened or alone.

Day Seventeen

"Amazingly, I Feel Saved"

Being single during Lent brings a tremendous blessing: an opportunity to repent, rejoice, recommit, and renew one's life and spirituality.

I believe God spares me and gives me time to welcome wholeheartedly whichever future partner He's preparing for me.

For 12 years I was engaged to a non-believer. I kept my faith and prayer that somehow, someday, he would be able to see God's grace, compassion, and blessings through me and our relationship. It ended recently, due to his refusal to receive the sacrament of matrimony, after we had decided to get married. It was totally the opposite of my principle.

So here I am, becoming single again.

It is my first Lent single after more than a decade of engagement. Amazingly, I feel saved.

Surely, I feel that something is missing in my life. However, Lent has invited me to reflect on the meaning of being a Catholic – not only in status and prayer but as something consistently held in my heart.

I wouldn't exchange what I believe for anything. Lent gives me strength to move on, forgive, and keep the faith, hoping that God will eventually send me a true partner – not only in life but also in faith.

This Lent I lift up my gratitude to the Lord, who has preserved, protected, and guarded me. In His salvation, I shall be reborn – and so I surrender. I let Him use my heart, my soul, my everything to spread His love and grace.

Thank You, Father. Thy will be done.

——◆——

Father, my faith is Your gift to me. Let me spend this holy season in a constant state of gratitude. Through my prayers, the sacrifices I make, and my service of others, preserve me in Your love and safeguard my heart. Let all that I believe and every experience of Your love enrich my life so that it may better express Your grace, Your compassion, and Your incessant blessings. Let me wholeheartedly recommit myself to Your Son so that He can use my heart to spread His love, grace, and peace.

Day Eighteen

"Single Life, Followed by Easter Joy"

Lent is a time for extra prayer and penance, meditation on the sufferings of Christ, and longing for the glory of the resurrection.

Being single and seeking a spouse with whom to find fulfillment is also a penance and something that motivates me to pray more. It is a cross to accept and even embrace, not just the celibacy required of me, but above all, the intimate friendship and companionship that a wife would bring, which I now lack.

Although Christ was never without His Father in heaven, He chose to experience in His human nature the desolation and spiritual agony of being abandoned by the Father while He was on the cross. Like Jesus, I am sometimes tempted to say, "My God, my God, why have You abandoned me?

Why have You left me alone when I feel a great longing for a good wife?"

But then my faith tells me that, indeed, God is always with me, that I should trust that He knows what is best for me, that this small Lenten sacrifice of living a single life, at least for the time allotted for me in God's plan, is good for me. It purifies me spiritually and inspires me to pray more and trust more in divine providence.

I pray that God may grant me the grace to always embrace His holy will as Christ and Our Lady did and to trust that my Lenten penance of single life will be followed by Easter joy with that one special woman they have chosen especially for me.

———⊰✦⊱———

Almighty God, I pray that the hardship I experience and the loneliness I often feel will be a suitable offering to You this Lenten season. Let me especially embrace the penances I do not chose, the ones that nonetheless can bind me more intimately with the suffering of Your Son and His death on the cross. Through my willingness to accept that You alone know what is truly best for me, may I experience the joy of the risen Christ with heart and mind renewed by the light of His glory.

Day Nineteen

"Let Us Fast from Comparisons"

"I don't think people realize how irreplaceable they are," one of the religious sisters I lived with told me one night.

Although she made that comment almost two years ago, I revisit the message daily: We truly are gifts. Perhaps this Lent we can feast on our giftedness while fasting from comparing ourselves to others.

What does it mean to be a gift?

It means, first of all, going to that place of solitude, the place of transformation where we encounter our vulnerabilities and wounds. It means, then, that we go into the desert with Jesus, just as He did before he began His ministry. It requires us to come to that place where we have nothing to prove and to simply allow ourselves to be loved. It means embracing our humanity just as Jesus did – weaknesses and all.

Thus, it can only be life-giving if we reverence our uniqueness. One of the best ways to do this is to not compare our state of life, successes, or weaknesses with those of others. There is absolutely no room for competition in the Kingdom of God.

This means not comparing the gift that I am to the gift that anyone else is – and finding joy in that truth. It means reminding ourselves that when our gift is not accepted the way we may want it to be, our worth is in no way decreased. It means seeing everyone I encounter as teachers – and intentionally thanking them for revealing to me the deep truths of myself.

So together let us fast from the temptation to compare and instead feast on gratitude for the gifts that we are and that we are in the process of becoming.

Is this specific to a spirituality of singleness?

Not necessarily. But it is unequivocally part of a spirituality of single-mindedness to the Spirit, which still persists long after we have found someone.

⇒◆⇐

Lord Jesus, Your 40 days in the desert call us to a place of solitude wherein we rediscover just what a gift each life is and how precious we are in the mind and heart of the Father. Let me accept His love throughout these 40 days so that I can see and love in others what the Father sees and loves in me. Help me accept and celebrate my humanity as You did, knowing that the Father uses even my fragility, weakness, and sin for His redemptive purposes. Keep me single-minded in my openness to Your Spirit and open-minded in my recognition of the giftedness of others.

Day Twenty

"Single Life Is Not a Barren Spiritual Desert"

This time of year, the question inevitably arises: "What have you given up for Lent?"

As a child, my answer was chocolate. When I stopped eating meat, I'd joke that I would give up vegetarianism for Lent. Later, my ex-fiancé and I abstained from kissing – remembering, of course, that Sundays don't count!

But growing older, I've learned the value in focusing less on what to give up and more on what I choose to embrace.

Last month I turned 40. Forty is a significant number in Scripture. The flood rained down for 40 days, the Israelites wandered in the desert for 40 years, and Jesus endured 40 days in the wilderness. Now we journey through 40 days of Lent.

"Single Life Is Not a Barren Spiritual Desert"

At times I've viewed my 40 years of singleness as a cross to be endured. I sometimes focus on what I don't have as a single woman rather than the unique blessings of this season of life.

But the single life is not defined as a barren spiritual desert, as simply a holding ground before reaching the promised land of marriage. Rather, it can be a flourishing time of fruitfulness, connection, and community. It certainly was that for Jesus.

A desert is a place with little precipitation. Deserts can look very different, from Antarctica to the Sahara. Likewise, spiritual deserts occur in all states of life, married or single. We singles may be more attuned to our own particular burdens of loneliness or longing, but everyone experiences them.

During seasons of dryness, we can choose to respond with hope. Believing that my best days are ahead, I open myself to God working His perfect plan for my life. Whether I marry someday or remain single, Jehovah Gyra, the God who provides, is Himself more than I'll ever need.

⋙◆⋘

Father of our Lord Jesus Christ, there is nothing I could ever give You that would be a fitting acknowledgment of all that You have given me. Let me therefore embrace each one of these 40 days for what they are meant to be: opportuni-

ties to be drawn more intimately into the mystery of Your redeeming love. Let each of my offerings express my gratitude and all my actions reflect the sacrificial giving of Your Son.

Day Twenty-One

"I Want to Seek First the Kingdom of God"

When you're single and 30, being unattached is always a challenge. However, there is something about the Lenten season that helps me see this challenge in a unique light.

As Lent began, I was counting down to my 31st birthday. It would be easy (and convenient) to think more about my upcoming birthday than to honor Jesus' 40 days in the wilderness.

But I know this is not God's will for me. I want to commit myself to trusting God with my future mate more than ever and truly "seek first the Kingdom of God" (Matthew 6:33).

For any male readers who are in a similar position, I'd like to share a few things that have been helpful to me.

Receiving the Eucharist often has been hugely beneficial. The Body and Blood of Jesus is true manhood for any man who's committed to living sexually pure and treating his body as a temple of the Holy Spirit.

A life of daily prayer, along with reading and meditating on the Word of God, are also important.

In addition, staying connected to a Spirit-filled Catholic Church is vital.

Finally, have a Catholic accountability partner with whom you can share your spiritual struggles and goals, praying for each other. Spend at least half an hour a week talking to this person.

What better time than Lent to get radically committed to trusting God as a single man? This time of year is about something much deeper than abstaining from meat once a week. It's about being open to the transformative work that God, through the Holy Spirit, wants to do in the depths of the heart.

⸺◈⸺

Heavenly Father, throughout these 40 days, let me entrust myself more completely to Your Holy Spirit. Through frequent reception of the Eucharist, reflection on Your Word, and a renewed commitment to being engaged with other members of Christ's body, conform my mind and heart more completely to that of Your Son. At the end of Lent let me emerge with the resurrected Christ as the man You have created me to be, so that others may come to accept their place within Your kingdom.

Day Twenty-Two

"Love Is Healing"

As ashes are placed on my forehead at the beginning of each Lenten season, I find renewed hope and peace in the unique call that God has set on my heart. The Lenten journey is meaningful for all Catholics, but as a single 20-something, Lent offers me a special opportunity to re-dedicate myself to the One who holds me close to His heart.

I may not understand His timing or His purpose, but I can learn to trust in the path He has laid before me. God promises to walk the difficult path of single life beside me, and I know He holds my hand as I face each day, each task, and each event. I long for a strong, faithful companion, and I know that God uses the season of Lent to remind me that He is the strong, faithful companion I long for.

Just as Jesus spent 40 days in the desert, my Lenten journey is a daily pilgrimage to Easter, a daily recommitment to my faith and my hope that God will recreate me in each season of life into the person He wants me to be: a better daughter, friend, and future wife.

To me, Lent is a season of healing – healing from my sins, my doubts, and the temptations of this world. God's healing power is found in focused prayer, dedicated fasting, and thoughtful almsgiving, all hallmarks of our Lenten journey. God's love flows through this season, renewing my soul for the joy of Easter and all that is to come.

Love is healing, and there is nothing more powerful than that.

Father, the Season of Lent is a gift for Your holy people, a time to unite our lives with the life of Your Son. Through the disciplines of Lent may we learn from Christ, who has entered in to the desert experiences of our lives, and walk with Him the way that leads to resurrected glory.

Day Twenty-Three

"I'm Rolling with the Dating Disappointments"

Being a young Catholic single in Chicagoland has brought many challenges over the years. I am currently 36 and have been searching for a good-quality Catholic lady since I was 20.

I have attended many events for 20- and 30-somethings: Theology On Tap, Yacht Club, ALPHA, game nights, movie nights, retreats, Spirit & Truth, praise and worship, meet-up groups, fundraisers, oil-painting classes, dance nights, and other socials.

I have met and dated some great ladies; however, we did not coagulate. Either I was interested in her and she was not interested in me, or she was interested in me and I was not interested in her.

I have been a member of CatholicMatch for more than

six years and have not found the right mate yet, but I believe this service is a great way to meet some quality Catholics, so keep the faith during your journey.

After learning about Pope John Paul's Theology of the Body, I have come to appreciate his work and those who have answered his call to spread the word. I met some impressive ladies who have made wonderful spouses for my friends.

It is true when people say that if you want a good laugh, make plans and then see what plans God has for you.

This Lent, I'm trying to place more trust in His plans. I'm rolling with the dating disappointments and looking for the positives. I know His grace surrounds me every day.

Loving Father, I know that my life is enveloped by Your generous love. Even in the midst of challenges and disappointments I always discover joy and peace when letting go of my plans in place of Yours. Through the disciplines of Lent give me, like Jeremiah, a "well-trained tongue" so I can better spread Your word and be an encouragement to those who have lost their way to You.

Day Twenty-Four

"Why Am I Still Single?"

It is all too easy to find myself asking, even pleading, with God: "Why am I still single?"

Not long ago I would kneel in church before and after Mass, begging God to let me get married soon. The majority of my prayer life centered on the topic of my singleness.

After some less than perfect dates and some perfect-on-paper relationships, I started to withdraw from the dating scene. It was then I was able to hear what God was telling me and grow closer to Him.

I look at Lent less as a time to dwell on singleness and more of a time to reflect on Christ's pure love for His people.

It is so easy to get caught up in the why-me feelings of being single, but why not spend this Lent growing closer to God and renewing your faith? Why not spend your time praying for your future spouse and children? Remember, putting yourself first is likened to worshiping false prophets or idols.

I attended a wedding right before Lent, and the priest said that in order to find true joy, you need to take the letters of "joy" apart and check your priorities: If your priorities are Jesus, Others, and then You, you're on a good path!

May this Lenten season bring you the time to reflect on Jesus' selfless love and the peace to know that if you have a strong calling, God will provide.

I close with one of my favorite Bible verses, John 15:7: "If you remain in Me and My words remain in you, ask whatever you wish, and it will be given you."

———◆———

Lord Jesus, be always at the center of my prayers. Keep my vision pure in order that I may always see You first, then others, and lastly myself. Let this alone give me the joy and peace that is Your gift to the world. Throughout these 40 days let me draw ever closer to You so that Your word will remain in me and all my asking will be selfless, as was the gift of Your bruised and broken body on the Cross.

Day Twenty-Five

"Keep Doing What You're Doing"

The first Lent after I became single again, money was as scarce as was hope for the future. The Lenten tradition is to give up something, but there wasn't anything else I could give – all had been taken from me anyway, or so it seemed.

I decided to contribute instead, somehow multiplying a small donation.

As a child I learned to crochet. It always brought me joy to make things. I knew our local anti-abortion clinic gives away baby booties to expecting moms, so, with a burst of Lenten inspiration, I bought some yarn and started crocheting.

The first few were simple but later became more creative with blue ribbons and pink roses. I made one pair each evening. It was relaxing, lifting my mind off my problems. That Lent I donated 40 pairs of booties. What a great feeling!

As single Catholics, sometimes we need to be more proactive in seeking sources of meaning and purpose. In this Lenten gig, I had found one. I have continued crocheting, donating by now more than 800 pairs.

Three years ago, while paused at an intersection, I noticed a car alongside mine: a woman driving two boys who were laughing and playing. From the rearview mirror hung a pair of baby booties – a pair I had made!

A surge of adrenaline rushed from my toes to my ears, wanting to jump out and ask if the booties were her son's or another child she was pregnant with. Instead I just sat motionless, overcome with emotion.

As the light turned green, we went on our ways, never crossing paths again.

That day God gave me a gift, saying, "Keep doing what you're doing; it does make a difference."

I never met any of the children whose lives were spared because a scared pregnant woman was given a pair of baby booties, a dainty symbol of the beautiful life inside her. But God knows who they are, and that's all that matters.

⤜◆⤐

Lord, sometimes I feel as if there isn't much that I can do to spread Your word or advance the growth of Your kingdom in the world. While I do believe that You weave all things together for the good of those who love You, sometimes I doubt the effectiveness of my little tokens of love and sacrifice. Help me see beyond my own limited perspective. Give me a new horizon that will keep me focused on the difference I can make; give me the courage to keep on doing what I'm doing.

Day Twenty-Six

"One of Those Moments That Lasts a Lifetime"

I recently traveled to Shanghai on business and was dropped off at the front of the international terminal. As the van pulled in, I saw a woman – a beggar who at some point in her life had been severely burned. Her face was deeply scarred and she had the use of only three fingers on each hand.

It was a busy morning, and I have to admit: She was something I personally didn't want to deal with. My first instinct was to go into the terminal and just avoid the situation.

But then another, stronger instinct kicked in, and I knew without a doubt that wasn't the Christian response. I pulled out some money and gave it to her. She bowed to me and thanked me in Chinese several times.

For a moment our eyes met...and it was one of those moments that seems to last a lifetime. I wondered if I hadn't just seen the face of Jesus.

As we stepped out of the van, I asked my coworker if he had seen her. He had not and had no idea what I was talking about. When I turned to look back for her, I could no longer see her on the platform. Why did I see her and my colleague did not?

As Catholics during Lent, we're challenged to make a true and total change in our direction along the path of life. At times that change forces us to stand against a strong current that conflicts with what we're bombarded with through so many mediums and people.

As single people seeking significant others or religious vocations, we are called to see the value of people beyond some pleasure or benefit we might receive from them. We're each challenged to pursue a common good greater than ourselves.

May God grant us wisdom for the journey.

⊰⬩⊱

Lord God, after we had sinned, You did not avoid our situation but through Your prophets promised to restore what we lost when we rejected Your friendship. In the fullness of time You sent Your Son so You could look us in the eyes and see a love that is far greater than ourselves. Help me to keep my eyes fixed upon the face of Jesus so that I can see the goodness, truth, and beauty in myself and in all those I meet.

Day Twenty-Seven

"For Once I See Single Life as a Blessing"

My first Bible arrived in the mail two days ago.

Until that point it hadn't occurred to me that I had never acquired my own Bible. Growing up we had the family Bible, but eventually I left home to begin my life in the world.

Along with my Bible, I decided to also get a Bible study guide; it was obvious I had much to learn.

Being a 26-year-old single Catholic woman with a new fascination with theology and apologetics, I am grateful for this Lent, a season when I am inching my way closer and closer to our Lord through the Eucharist and through Scripture.

What better way to increase my proximity to the Lord Almighty God this Lent than daily Mass and Eucharist? How blessed we are as Catholics to have the privilege to stand in front of the actual Body of Christ, to eat His flesh as He instructed us to do so!

Jesus tells us in John 6:35: "I am the bread of life; whoever comes to Me will never hunger and whoever believes in Me will never thirst."

The way to the Bread of Life is the Catholic Church, and through this Church we have the opportunity to be truly and completely forgiven of all sins. We are given the chance to repent and start anew.

If that's not unconditional love, I do not know what is.

For once I feel my life single is a blessing, as my heart and soul are focused on inviting the Holy Spirit to lead me down the path chosen for me. I feel at peace with God's plan for me, even though I do not yet know it.

———⊰◦⊱———

Heavenly Father, open my heart to receive Your Word so that throughout these 40 days I may move ever closer to You. Let the "bread come down from heaven," be the food that sustains me as I fast from everything that keeps me from hungering for You. Let me rest in that peace which comes from following Your plan for my life with confidence and joy.

Day Twenty-Eight

"The Depths of My Sins Were Forgiven"

Lent is the penitential period that guided my return to our Father's house. I had abandoned my Catholic faith for 33 years. Like the prodigal son, I was feeding on the husks the pigs ate. Darkness surrounded me while buried in the crypt of sin. The cleaves of humiliation cut deep into my heart.

Faith is the answer He sent while I grappled with a plank of conversion and repentance. The Lenten season of 2004 introduced my second plank, reconciliation and penance, rescuing me from the darkest depths of transgression.

But pride and ego made it difficult to ask for forgiveness. How could I have let this go on for so long?

I was lost, stumbling on a path potholed with alcohol, lust, and self-gratification. The squall on the horizon exploded, and the storm in my soul sank me. I was shipwrecked, holding to a plank floating in the open sea.

I believe Mary the Blessed Virgin and St. Paul were by my side as I floated aimlessly on this destitute board. Clinging to my piece of wood, Mary clutched me from the storm.

"Do as He tells you," she said, leading me to her Son.

His mercy is unfathomable, and the depths of my sins were forgiven. Light overcame darkness, my sins were forgiven, and grace restored.

Lent is a time of reflection on our storms, and penance is our port. The sacrament of reconciliation restored God's grace in me. I became intimate with Him and sat at His table, feasting at the banquet of the Holy Eucharist with our community, the Church.

I offer my Lenten journey of sacrifice for our pope, bishops, priests, sisters, lay missioners, and the lost souls of poor sinners. I am so grateful to have made the journey back home.

———◆———

Father of Mercy, let the light of Your Son reach into the darkness that overwhelms and incapacitates so many of Your children. By Your holy light lead them into the safe harbor of Your unfathomable love, to feast at the table of the Eucharist and to be reunited once again with the company of friends that constitute Christ's body, the Church.

Day Twenty-Nine

"I Need Lots of Prayer and Encouragement"

Lent can be a lonely journey as a single person, just as our Lord Jesus experienced. I am grateful for the kindness and support of my wonderful friends, but there comes that time every day when I must return to my aloneness in my home.

Having had a committed partner for nearly 40 years, adjusting to this lonely life wasn't easy – especially since my husband was suddenly taken from me. Overwhelmed is the best description of my feelings the first several months of my loss.

Dan and I were such a close couple that we held hands in church during the homily. He was a tremendous help with housework, yard work, and handling so many things in our marriage. What a shock to take on all the responsibilities overnight.

As a single person, it is sometimes difficult to feel motivated to accomplish all the chores that need attending to. Music and spiritual reading help, but I feel I need a lot of prayer and encouragement (and mind games at times!) to get me going.

This season I am trying to focus more on what Jesus endured during the 40 days that became the first Lenten season. He must have felt rejected, alone, hungry, and exhausted. There were times when He wondered if his Father had left Him or heard His disappointments, temptations, and suffering.

My prayer is that Jesus will give me strength to move forward and eagerly await my new life in Pittsburgh. I am grateful for many blessings and the opportunity to be closer to my children and grandchildren.

Leaving my Florida friends behind will be bittersweet. I am looking forward to rekindling my friendships in the Pittsburgh area and, most especially, meeting new people – both men and women.

I do believe there may be another exceptional someone out there intended just for me. I'm trusting in answered prayers.

———◆———

Lord Jesus, the purpose of Your time in the desert is only properly understood when we willingly embrace the feelings of rejection and loneliness that befall us unexpectedly. When we most hunger for that for which our hearts long, we can exhaust ourselves by the futile ways we seek to satisfy them. Teach me Your desert wisdom so that I can move through these 40 days more closely united to You and Your Father's will.

Day Thirty

"Maybe We Can Still Put God First"

The Lenten season is the most profound one in my life. This is when God's love is almost tangible for me.

Just last week, I was reading my diary entry from 2005. I was doing great; I had a great-paying job, my own place, and close friends around me.

Strangely, these days those entries sound different. I wasn't very happy at work, and God was just something between social engagements. I practically became involved in the parish so I could see friends. I was missing the point.

Today, without a significant job, I am blessed by what I have. With fewer friends but more family, I am enriched daily by God's teachings. I spend time adoring Him in the Blessed Sacrament after daily Mass.

People who knew me before might think that my life had turned for the worst, but my love for God has doubled compared with those so-called happy days in the past.

So, has my life gone kaput?

Admittedly, I might not do all these things when working, and I'd be more likely to put God second or third in my life. Should we wait for adversity to strike before we adore God?

In between our many commitments and to-dos, maybe we can still put God first, to feel His unfathomable love for us.

This Lent, I am realizing how much I need God within me. Each time I receive the Eucharist, I carry Him inside me. I try to let His love shine through. I put it into practice every day, though I fail more than not. Still, there is God's grace, which compels me to keep trying and to love Him even more and more.

———✦———

Good and gracious God, I am grateful You remain present to us in the Holy Eucharist, to nourish our lives and embolden us to manifest Your love in the real circumstances of our lives. The abundance of Your love is the perfect antidote to the abundance celebrated by our culture and sought after by so many of Your sons and daughters, including me. Through the disciplines of Lent show me how to make greater room for You so I can adore You in all Your works and praise You with a pure heart.

Day Thirty-One

"Now I Feel No Sense of Urgency"

Reflecting upon the change from marriage to widowhood, I can trace the evolution of the thought process that brings me to the here and now. When I recovered from the worst of my grieving period, I was eager to find another "right one," so I set out on this venture, which included joining CatholicMatch.

Now I feel no sense of urgency. How did this come about? As time marched on, I became involved in more activities – some family, some social, and others that are Church or charity oriented. With increasing interest and involvement in these activities, I've discovered a sense of fulfillment…in a different way, of course.

Lent is an opportune time to work with the Church and charitable groups even more intensely, focusing upon some of the beatitudes and God's greatest commandments.

Being single I can offer more time in the service of our fellow man. It's a way to fulfill my present calling, and I regard serving as a privilege.

Being of service can easily be done here on Catholic-Match. Daily we see CatholicMatch members facing challenges. How helpful we can be to reach out with an encouraging word or prayer to bring them comfort.

I regard Lent as a time of joy. Why? It's a strong reminder of why our Lord put us here and the good we can do by sacrificing for others.

Also, despite the sufferings of Jesus, miracles took place – the Eucharist was instituted, and the prophecy of the resurrection was fulfilled. How can we not be thankful for what we have been given? How can we not show it? It's our calling!

—————

Lord Jesus, during Your time in the desert there was no sense of urgency to "be about Your Father's will." Instead, You took time to commune with Him. You emptied Yourself in order to be filled with the words that satisfy better than bread, to bow low before the Lord of heaven on earth, and to test Your resolve to fulfill the Father's plan to reconcile us to Himself. Let me go into the desert with You these 40 days, knowing it is a privilege and an opportunity, a time to feed, to worship, and to test my own resolve to love and to serve.

Day Thirty-Two

"It's a Yearly Checkpoint"

As a child and young adult, I knew Lent was a holy time, whether or not I gave up something I loved as a sacrifice.

The seasonal rules were all for good reasons: letting go of selfish desires, giving to the needy, and taking the time to reflect on past mistakes.

It's like a yearly checkpoint, a chance to hold myself accountable if the path I'm on has wandered from my understanding of God's will for me through the practice of my Catholic faith, a time to gauge if I'm closer to the life of service, joy, and peace I wish to lead rather than the enticing but empty ways of the world.

Now Lent is a key part of the solid foundation on which I seek to build a new relationship after a brief, disappointing marriage that was Catholic in name but not in commitment.

If Lent is observed in truth within an intimate partnership, then we can joyfully proclaim that we are alive in Christ on Easter Sunday, conquering the darkness of the tomb.

Resurrection will happen when we put Him in charge of our life choices and at the center of our world, rather than seek perfection or fulfillment in ourselves or any other human being.

Forgiveness, openness, patience, and tolerance are virtues I hope to grow this season with God's grace and Mary's intercession.

⥤◆⥢

Almighty Father, the pathway of these 40 days should lead us to a greater understanding of just what it means that the tomb was empty. We move throughout Lent eager to be ever more alive in the risen Christ, Whose death put an end to sin and gave the world a new and definitive horizon. Help me to stay on the pathway that leads to this discovery. Keep me safe from all the world's empty enticements that lead to a dark grave from which I could never arise.

Day Thirty-Three

"I Want to Spend More Time in Gratitude"

This Lent, along with giving up the usual sweets and spending more time in prayer, I decided to do something a little different. I wanted to spend more time in gratitude for all the wonderful things God has given me.

As a pastoral minister, I am blessed to have many wonderful parishioners who inspire me daily. This past year I was struck by how many couples in my parish celebrated 40 or 50 years of marriage. I realized how blessed I am to have such wonderful examples of couples living out the sacrament of marriage in my midst.

This Lent I decided to take a couple from my parish each day and to pray for them and their intentions, while also thanking God for the example and hope they give me as a single person. They show me what it truly means to live out their sacramental vows. They help me realize what I strive for one day in my own life.

There are so many couples who have blessed my life. From the young couple with small children, who make it a priority to come to Mass weekly, to the couple relying on each other while facing the uncertainty of illness to the couple who has been married for 72 years. They continue to inspire me.

I pray that this Lent my eyes will be opened a bit more not only to the ways I can grow closer to God but to the many ways God is working through His people – and specifically through the couples surrounding me who serve God, their families, and each other every day. What a great lesson to be reminded of this Lent.

———◆———

Eternal Father, the greatness of Your love has been revealed in the passion, death, and resurrection of Your Son. Through His Paschal Mystery we have been reunited with You and with one another. Through the communion we share in Christ's body, we are called to inspire, encourage, celebrate, correct, and cherish one another. Let my heart overflow with gratitude for all that Christ accomplishes for us and for His love at work in those around me.

Day Thirty-Four

"Am I Going to Find Someone at All?"

Why does the one person I'm interested in not seem interested in me?

I meet women who are attractive, or fun, or interesting, or devout, but why can't I meet someone who's all-in-one? I feel like my vocation is marriage, and I see so many people around me in good relationships or marriages.

Is there something wrong with me?

I'm getting older. Am I going find someone at all?

These are questions I've asked myself many times as a single person. I've felt frustrated, lonely, even a tad hopeless at times.

When I had my conversion six years ago, placing my trust in God was the hardest but most important thing I did. By surrendering all my anxieties, questions, and fears to Him and trusting Him to work out the details, I've experienced a deep peace in my life (and in hindsight, He's taken pretty good care of me as well).

But I recently came to the realization that I haven't been trusting Him in the dating area of my life. I have doubted that He'd really come through for me, that He'd answer my prayers, that He'd lead me (and another special someone) in the right direction, and that He'd bring the healing that I need in my life – all of this in order to begin living my vocation, which I believe is marriage.

So how to surrender?

A couple of Lents ago, I was vacuuming my bedroom and was struck by this thought: Jesus was on the cross, bleeding to death, when He cried out, "My God, My God, why have You abandoned Me?" It was very real and very dark. "God, where are You?"

But in His darkest moment, when He could not sense His Father, He still said, "Into Your hands I commend My spirit."

Wasn't this the most beautiful act of faith? Despite the worst pain and feeling of loneliness, He still stepped out.

If somehow I can unite my own questions, doubts, fears, and uncertainties to the ones He experienced – and then, in faith, echo His words of surrender – then I can bring this area of my life under His submission.

When I do that, I believe I'll be able to receive the blessings He wants to give me. I don't know exactly what that will entail, but I want to say yes and I believe He is good.

———◆———

Father, into Your hands I commend my own troubled, doubting, fragile, weak, and distrustful spirit; it's all that I have to offer You. This Lent I accept all that You have given me in Christ, and through the disciplines of this season I will surrender and submit myself to You. I will adhere to the same way walked by Christ when He gave Himself for me. I will stand faithfully at the foot of the Cross with Mary by my side. I will accompany Peter and John the morning they ran to the empty tomb. And I will sing Your praises all the days of my life.

Day Thirty-Five

"Do Not Judge by His Appearance"

The first reading for the fourth Sunday of Lent offered a good reminder of something we should consider when viewing CatholicMatch profiles that come into our queue. Check out 1st Samuel 16 for the complete reading, but here is the line that gave me a reason to say, "Sorry, God, I am guilty of that."

Samuel has gone to anoint a new king from one of Jesse's sons. He is sure that one very handsome son is the one God will choose.

Suddenly Samuel hears, "Do not judge by his appearance or from his lofty stature, because I have rejected him. Not as man sees does God see, because man sees the appearance, but the Lord looks into the heart."

The dictionary says that the word "judge" means to

form an estimate or evaluation of. I wonder how many dating profiles I have dismissed because the provided pictures just didn't make the member look like Robert Redford or some preconceived expectation in my head.

I dismissed bad lighting and poor camera skills and let that be the judge of whether or not I would make an attempt to contact them. It is not an easy thing to confess, but maybe you have found yourself doing that as well. I hope I am not the only guilty one!

My mom often used to say, "You can't judge a book by its cover."

I wonder if this book of Samuel is where the saying came from. It's something to think about this final week of Lent. May I not judge single men by their appearance, but instead invest the time needed to see the heart.

———————

Almighty Father, You peer into my heart and know me in a way I long to know myself. At the end of these 40 days let me see You more clearly, as You are, so that I may see myself and others as you do. Let my heart be cleansed and renewed by this holy season. May You become for me now and remain forever the lens by which I look upon the world.

Day Thirty-Six

"This Seclusion Is Preparation for a Great Love"

"Love comes from prayer, and prayer comes from remaining in seclusion."

ST. ISAAC OF SYRIA

As I look at this phrase, I tend to dismantle it piece by piece. I think it is one of the best ways to describe the origin of love, because prayer is all about coming into relationship with God and, as St. John tells us, "God is love."

It makes sense, then, that prayer increases our capacity for love – for the more we come to know God, who is love, the more we come to know what true love is.

The second part goes, "and prayer from remaining in seclusion." This is an interesting concept to wrap one's mind around. I know that personally some of my most productive prayer time is alone with the Lord in adoration. This seclusion eventually forces me to look inward and assess my own weaknesses and my utter inability to do anything pleasing to God without His grace.

Seclusion and prayer are like an intricate dance; each one helps the other out, like a couple doing a waltz. The ultimate result is something absolutely beautiful. As of late, I've been wrestling with this single state of life. In a sense I am secluded.

This leads me to consider what God said of Adam: "It is not good for the man to be alone. I will make a suitable partner for him" (Gen 2:18). We all know what God was thinking, but I wonder what it was like for Adam?

He really was secluded; there was no other rational human being for him to even converse with. Imagine what his prayer must have been like! All he had was God. The prayer born out of that type of seclusion must have been phenomenal. And at that point, he hadn't sinned. Man! His prayer and love must have been out of this world!

Maybe all of us in the single state of life should take note of this and not wallow in our seclusion but instead allow it to cultivate in us a powerful prayer life, thus developing a more powerful capacity to love. This seclusion is only the preparation for a great love for whomever God has destined for me.

Father, by my efforts alone I could never hope to please You, but You satisfy my desire to do so through the grace of Your Son. To understand this mystery of love, I must withdraw to a quiet and secluded place to converse with You. This reciprocity of giving and receiving fills my being with an overwhelming urge to express and share love, just as You express and share Your love with me. Let me withdraw these 40 days into the secluded recesses of my heart and experience prayer as it was meant to be from the beginning.

Day Thirty-Seven

"God Will Allow Me Contentment"

Ahh, this wonderful world we live in. Everywhere I go, everything I see, it's all about me.

I am youthful, but not young. I struggle to lose those pounds. I have wrinkles and a few unsightly age spots. And everyone – every company, every store and every manufacturer – is vowing to make me, the modern single woman, perfect. Perfectly beautiful, perfectly sexy, perfectly skinny, and perfectly desirable. Here's looking at me.

It's quite a message to receive from so many sources 365 days of the year.

But I like to shake it up a bit.

For 40 straight days every spring, I stop looking at me and remember to look within me. I seek a quiet peace within myself that is only possible in prayer. God, the One who created me, with all my wrinkles and bulges, will allow me contentment in everything I am if I just take the time to reflect with Him.

This Lent I've said the rosary or attended daily Mass or a Taizé service. I've read spiritually uplifting literature and concentrated on keeping my thoughts and attitudes positive. And of course I've given something up in the tradition of Lent.

I appreciate Lenten offerings as an outward reminder of the greater sacrifices that Christ made for me. But within me, it is more. It is the hush of a quiet chapel, the relief of a long reprieve, the swell of a great love, the assurance of an unbreakable trust. It is how God loves me. I can feel it.

Lent is a time to renew my ability to rise above those forceful cultural pressures to be perfect. And all the fulfillment is mine – even when I'm not wearing a dab of makeup.

⟾⬧⟸

Lord, for 40 straight days You invite us to look within ourselves for the assurance of Your love and a contentment the world cannot give. Through the gift of Your Spirit help me to accept and be faithful to Your invitation in order that I may be renewed in mind and heart by the sacrificial love of Your Son.

Day Thirty-Eight

"I Can Think Less About My Timeline"

I know someone who is perfect.

It's not me and it's not the man I hope to marry someday. It's Jesus Christ.

He chose to suffer humiliation, torture, and eventually death on the cross for my imperfections. His life was perfectly aligned with the will of the Father. Even though it meant unknown pain, He accepted it all to give us the hope of eternity with Him.

So even though being single may be the furthest thing from what I would choose for myself, I know God sees perfectly the plan He has for me and my future husband.

The season of Lent has been a chance to surrender more fully to His will for me. Instead of grasping for what

I want, I've tried to instead focus on prayerfully discerning what God wants me to do with this time of singleness. What is He trying to build in me in order to become a godly wife and mother?

I can choose to think less about my timeline and more about enjoying these moments. I know that in the future I will be able to look back and understand why I am single now and why I went through the experiences I have had.

The journey towards marriage can be difficult sometimes, but I always have hope – hope in a perfect God.

⋙◆⋘

Lord Jesus, the perfection of Your love has been revealed to us through the humiliation, torture, and death You endured. On the way marked out for us, the pain and suffering we sometimes experience results from trying to control or hurry Your Father's plan. This Lent renew within me the same hope You carried in Your heart while carrying the Cross upon Your shoulders. Let me embrace the journey I am on with the same confidence that enabled You to rise triumphant from the grave.

Day Thirty-Nine

"I Search for Love Even More Ardently"

Good Friday has arrived!

I am still single and alone, but I do grow closer to God at this holy time of the year.

Throughout Lent I've read more spiritual literature and spent more time in prayer, all while relishing the warmer weather and the many signs of spring. They make my heart grow fonder, and I search for love even more ardently. Spring is my favorite season, a season of love.

But I'm not searching for fleeting affection. I only search for true love and the only way is to follow and believe in all the teachings of our faith. Through the readings of Pope John Paul II's Theology of the Body, I now fully understand what true love is. (It's a must-read.)

My true love is coming soon, and I am looking forward to the greatest happiness in my remaining years. It is a time of sweet anticipation, as I await my annulment and dream of my future.

I have embraced Lent, making room for more closeness with God. It was been a time for the sacrament of penance, for yet another beginning.

Tonight, as we reflect on the ultimate sacrifice Jesus made for us, I am filled with love and gratitude. So much joy awaits us.

—◆—

Heavenly Father, the way of fulfillment requires the willingness on my part to begin again, the willingness to trust in Your mercy by rejecting what is false and clinging to what is good. The disciplines of this season have guided my actions, formed my thoughts, and helped secure my heart in the joy that springs from the loving sacrifice of Your Son. Stay with me through the end of these days even as I already long to sing "Alleluia."

Day Forty

"That Longing Remains"

Forty days in the wilderness. Forty days without food or drink. Forty days alone.

I've often wondered what was the hardest part for Jesus: the temptations, the hunger or thirst, the total solitude.

For me Lent involves a bit of all three: the temptation to give in and sneak some meat on a Friday; fasting from my favorite desserts; giving up meals on Ash Wednesday and Good Friday. And then there's the solitude. I've been single for the last three years, and that desire to share my life – my joys, my struggles, my God – with someone has only increased over time.

Working in the field of youth ministry, I often think about how nice it would be to come home after a long day with the teens and share with my husband how God was at work that day or about how confused I am or just to ask for prayers.

I'm grateful to have some incredible friends and a supportive family, and I know that my solitude is nothing like Jesus'. Nevertheless, that longing remains.

For Jesus – a man and God of intense relationships – I'm prone to think that the solitude was the worst. Did He miss His mother and father? Did He long for the company and laughter of the disciples?

Yet amidst those longings, Jesus had the most intimate relationship with God the Father, bonded by the Holy Spirit, and it was this relationship that sustained Him. He clung to the Father in prayer, offering up each day (and down the road, His very death) as an expression of His love and service.

This is what Lent is about for me. Whatever temptation, whatever deprivation, whatever loneliness I may feel, I want those things to push me closer into the embrace of my Father. Without that, an increased dependence on God, it's all for naught.

Forty days in the wilderness. Forty days without food or drink. Forty days alone. A cross of wood and the sins of the world. That is how much Jesus loves me. By God's grace and strength, may my own temptations, fasting, and solitude be a witness of my love for Him in return. And as we move into the Easter season, may this love continue to grow with the joy of Christ's resurrection. He is risen, and thus, we are never alone.

———⟫◦⟪———

Lord, at the conclusion of these 40 days, the longing for You remains. I know that the temptations You faced, the loneliness You experienced, and the hunger You felt lasted beyond Your time in the desert. I know the same will be true for me. But I also know that You fed on food not known, enjoyed the companionship of Your followers, and trusted always in Your Father's care. Let everything I have learned make it possible for me to do the same as I step out of this sacred time back into a world that is often more a wasteland than the deserted place to which You retreated.

Epilogue

"Join the Music of Heaven"

Music can open the human heart. It has a way even without words to pull out emotions that were once buried deep inside.

Music can lift our hearts to God. It doesn't even matter as to the type of music – pop, rock, swing, jazz, or classical – music reaches out to all people and speaks to them in language they can hear. Like music, prayer can set the stage for God to speak to the human heart.

These thoughts of music and prayer flood my mind as I consider what God has done for us in giving us His Son, Jesus – the perfect "Divine Song," as it were. Written by the Author of Life, the Lord God Almighty. Sung by His only Son. Backed up by the Holy Spirit. Easter is God's song of life! Now He wants us to join in the Easter song!

Lenten Reflections for Singles

Lent, like a well-worn tune, is once more come and gone. The Church gives it to us in order to take time to peel back the crusty layers of stuff that clog our spiritual ears. Easter is here, singing anew the notes of the risen Lord, "Jesus Christ is risen today!" The amazing Easter song that "God so loved the world that He gave his only Son, so that everyone who believes in Him might not perish but might have eternal life" are not empty lyrics; they sing of God's love for us, which calls us to new life in Christ.

If we accept the invitation, Jesus will bind us to Himself in the most intimate of life-giving relationships. This knowledge that Jesus wants a personal relationship with me is more than comforting. It is that which makes my heart sing! Admittedly, as a single woman, it also has the effect of providing me with a deep sense of reassurance: I really am loved more than I can imagine.

As we move into the 50 days of the Easter season, the Church asks us to reflect on and receive the Good News that Jesus took on our nature to show us the way to our Father. Jesus reveals the face of God, the one who loves us best. Jesus tells us who we are: precious, worth dying for, redeemed, loved. The Incarnate God, the Second Person of the Trinity, Jesus – He wants to share His risen life with each of us!

So now that Easter is here, how will you accept the invitation to sing with the risen Lord? Many of the saints of the

Church have offered good advice. Some have suggested that we practice a prayer of mindfulness of the sacred presence of Christ. This means that we not only look for our Lord throughout our day, but we also invite Him into all of our activities, even the most ordinary.

Another bit of advice to help us find our voice comes from a wise priest. He once told me to apply how we treat the ones we love to our relationship with Jesus: We think of them; we don't do anything to hurt them; and we spend time with them.

Do this with Jesus. Think often of Him. Live in His love. Sing His song in life. Act in ways that will delight Him. Do nothing that will hurt Him. Spend time with Jesus. Talk to Him in prayer. Meet Him in the Eucharist.

The Eucharist is, of course, where we come into direct contact with Jesus through word and sacrament. It is the best prayer of the Church. When we receive Jesus in Communion we are able to sing God's music full out. During Mass, if we focus all of our attention on Who it is that is coming "under our roofs," our communion will be more mindful, more loving.

Holy Communion is the most intimate of times when our Lord continues to touch, heal and speak to us in the deepest chambers of our heart. It is a profound moment of spiritual union. We may even continue this union through Eucharistic Adoration. This is where we spend time just loving Jesus.

Given the many responsibilities, challenges, and rewards that modern life offers, its music can be jarring and lacking in harmony. Facing life's challenges as a single person can also make life's music a bit more difficult to play. Singing God's song, however, is just the opposite – it really is that easy. Only peace, joy, and love are the notes He plays.

The Lord God's Easter song, sung by His only begotten Son, is an irresistible tune. It compels us to recommit ourselves to living with the Lord. It inspires us to open the doors of our heart wide to accepting the invitation to the divine sing-a-long. Let us join in the Heavenly chorus: Jesus Christ is risen today, Alleluia!

– Theresa Notare

BISHOP KEVIN C. RHOADES, the son of the late Charles and Mary Rhoades, was born Nov. 26, 1957, in Mahanoy City, Pennsylvania. He grew up in Lebanon, where he was a member of Assumption of the Blessed Virgin Mary Parish.

He enrolled at Mount St. Mary's College (now University) in Emmitsburg, Maryland, in the fall of 1975, and studied there for two years. In 1977 he entered St. Charles Borromeo Seminary in Overbrook, Pennsylvania, and earned a bachelor's degree in philosophy in 1979. He did his theological studies at the North American College and the Pontifical Gregorian University, both in Rome, from 1979-1983. He also studied Spanish at the University of Salamanca in Spain during the summer of 1982.

Cardinal Terence Cooke ordained Bishop Rhoades a deacon at St. Peter's Basilica in Vatican City in 1982. He was ordained a priest of the Harrisburg Diocese on July 9, 1983, by then-Auxiliary Bishop William Keeler. The ceremony took place at Assumption of the Blessed Virgin Mary Church in Lebanon and was the first ordination to take place in the county.

His first assignment in the diocese was as parochial vicar at St. Patrick Parish in York from 1983-1985. During this time, he also ministered in the Spanish-speaking apostolates at Cristo Salvador Parish in York and Cristo Rey Mission in Bendersville. In 1985 he returned to the Gregorian University in Rome, where he earned advanced degrees in dogmatic theology and canon law.

In 1988 he came back to the Harrisburg Diocese to serve as assistant chancellor under then-Bishop Keeler. During this time, he also ministered as the director of the Spanish apostolate in Dauphin, Cumberland and Perry counties, and as administrator pro-tem of Our Lady of Guadalupe Parish in Lebanon.

Bishop Rhoades was appointed pastor of St. Francis of Assisi Parish, Harrisburg, in 1990. He served there until 1995, when he accepted a full-time faculty position with Mount St. Mary's Seminary. While there, he taught courses in systematic theology, canon law and Hispanic ministry.

In March 1997 he was named rector of Mount St. Mary's Seminary, a role he fulfilled until his appointment by Pope John Paul II as bishop of the Diocese of Harrisburg on Oct. 14, 2004.

He was ordained a bishop on Dec. 9, 2004, by Cardinal Justin Rigali, archbishop of Philadelphia. On that date he began his ministry as bishop of Harrisburg, Pennsylvania.

Bishop Rhoades was appointed the Ninth Bishop of the Diocese of Fort Wayne-South Bend, Ind., on Nov. 14, 2009, by Pope Benedict XVI, and installed on Jan. 13, 2010, in the Cathedral of the Immaculate Conception in Fort Wayne.

While serving as bishop of Harrisburg, Bishop Rhoades served as president of the Pennsylvania Catholic Conference and on the Board of Trustees of St. Charles Seminary, the Board of Regents of St. Vincent Seminary and the Board of Trustees of Mount St. Mary's University.

Currently Bishop Rhoades serves as chair of the United States Conference of Catholic Bishops (USCCB) Committee on Laity, Marriage, Family Life, and Youth and as chair of the USCCB Task Force on Health Care. He serves as a member of the Administrative Committee of the USCCB, the National Advisory Council and the USCCB Committee on Doctrine. He also continues to assist as a member of the Board of Trustees of the Basilica of the National Shrine of the Immaculate Conception, the Episcopal Advisory Board of the Theology of the Body Institute, the Episcopal Cabinet of Catholic Charities USA, the Bishops' Advisory Council of the Institute for Priestly Formation, the Advisory Board of the National Conference of Diocesan Vocation Directors and the Advisory Board of the Augustine Institute.

On the international level, Bishop Rhoades serves as Catholic Co-Chair of the International Catholic-Reformed Theological Dialogue on behalf of the Pontifical Council for Promoting Christian Unity.

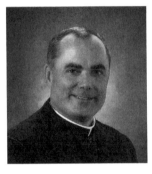

FATHER GARY C. CASTER is a priest of the diocese of Peoria, Ill., ordained in 1992. He began his studies for the priesthood at the Catholic University of America as a Basselin Scholar, graduating summa cum laude and Phi Beta Kappa with a bachelor's degree and licentiate in philosophy. He continued priestly formation at the North American College in Rome and Mount St. Mary's Seminary in Emmitsburg, Maryland, earning a master of divinity as well as a master's in Church history.

Fr. Caster began his priestly ministry as a high school chaplain and religion teacher at Peoria Notre Dame High School. He directed the religion department and helped put in place a prevention program for at-risk students. At the same time he worked with the Office of Family Life to develop a consistent program of marriage preparation and taught Church history and ecclesiology to the men in formation for the permanent diaconate. During this time, he published a collection of poems, wrote and produced shows for EWTN, including the popular *Angel Force*, and numerous times presented papers on the contribution of Catholic authors, especially Ms. Berry Morgan. Throughout this time, Fr. Caster continued to write articles on his favorite saint, Thérèse of Lisieux.

After Notre Dame High School, Fr. Caster became the director of campus ministry at the St. Robert Bellarmine

Newman Center, which serves Illinois State University and Illinois Wesleyan University. He was also instrumental in bringing campus ministry to Eureka College. Together with another priest of the diocese of Peoria, Father Stanley Deptula, he developed a pastoral program for students graduating from college who wanted to serve the local church as they continued their discernment. Students participating in the Sts. Titus and Timothy Pastoral Apostolate were placed in a variety of ministerial settings and have been an invaluable asset to the local Church. Quite a few have gone on to the priesthood and consecrated life.

After leaving St. Robert Bellarmine, Father Caster went to work for the bishop of Peoria doing special projects, which included traveling across the country to lead parish missions and retreats. He is the author of *Mary, In Her Own Words: The Mother of God in Scripture,* published by Servant Books in 2006, and *The Little Way of Lent: Meditations in the Spirit of St. Thérèse,* published in 2010 by Servant Books.

Currently Fr. Caster has returned to campus ministry in the diocese of Springfield, Massachuetts, as the Catholic chaplain of Williams College. Fr. Caster has contributed articles to various publications, including *Magnificat,* and continues to assist with EWTN shows, lead retreats, paint, write poetry and preach the Gospel. He welcomes the chance to speak about the Theology of the Body, the New Evangelization, the communion of saints, difficulties in the spiritual life and faith and culture.

THERESA NOTARE is a second generation Italian-American. Her mother was the last of 12 children and her father the fourth in a line of nine. Theresa grew up in New Jersey withtwo sisters and a brother.

Theresa earned a doctorate in church history in 2008 from the Catholic University of America in Washington, D.C. She has a master's in church history and theology from the Pacific School of Religion at the Graduate Theological Union at Berkeley, Calif. She has also studied at the Immaculate Conception Seminary in the Archdiocese of Newark, New Jersey. She completed her first post-secondary degree in 1979, graduating magna cum laude with a bachelor's degree in fine arts education from Montclair State College in UpperMontclair, New Jersey.

Theresa has taught religious education, art and pilates. She is trained in classical ballet and enjoys cooking, sewing and listening to classical music.

She serves in the Secretariat for the Laity, Marriage, Family Life & Youth at the United States Conference of Catholic Bishops in Washington, DC. Theresa is the assistant director of the bishops' Natural Family Planning Program. She provides consultation on programming issues to diocesan NFP coordinators, conducts research on human sexuality, chastity, marriage and fertility and also coordinates national seminars.

Theresa is a member of the Catholic Church Historical Society, the National Association of Catholic Family Life Ministers and the USCCB's Delegation to the 2012 World Congress on the Family, sponsored by the Pontifical Council for the Family. She also is a member of the Anglican-Roman Catholic ecumenical dialogue in the USA.

Success Stories

Wedding Bells in Easter

Something remarkable happens every single day here at CatholicMatch: We receive word from a former member who has just married or become engaged to someone he or she met on our website. Each "success story" (as we dub them) brings great joy to the CatholicMatch team. We credit the Holy Spirit, who does indeed work in mysterious ways – in cyberspace, in pews, on bended knee.

As we review these relationship archives, some themes emerge, like the role of prayer and the beauty of shared Eucharist. We hear from many members who folded their dating efforts into the Lenten journey. After all, isn't any budding relationship better off with prayer, almsgiving and fasting? The promise of Easter morning – like a wedding day – is the ultimate reward.

Here's an example.

When Brittany first joined CatholicMatch, the 20-something from Eastern Iowa selected just one profile to respond to: Dan.

The handsome 26-year-old from Omaha caught her eye, so she held her breath and sent him a smiling emoticon.

He responded eagerly, and they struck up a correspondence. Their first phone call went surprisingly well and was

quickly followed by plans to meet in. Dan made the trek to across Iowa to see Brittany on Nov. 14.

"She was gorgeous and I was surprised she would ever have wanted to say hello to me in the first place," he told CatholicMatch.

It only got better when he pulled into her driveway and found her even more beautiful in person.

Dan and Brittany both have old-fashioned values, and he approached her father to ask for his permission to court his daughter. "This was something Brittany and I greatly desired in order to ensure a holy and long-lasting traditional relationship," he said.

The Midwesterners saw each other as much as possible their first winter together. Come Lent, they committed to making the most of the season. It was a fruitful time for their budding relationship.

A year later, during Easter 2011, Dan had another question for Brittany's father: This time he asked permission to propose marriage. Brittany's dad considered it an honor to have Dan as a son-in-law and happily gave the green light.

On April 30 Brittany and Dan enjoyed a picnic in the park and then went to a cathedral, where they made a personal consecration of their courtship to the Immaculate Heart of Mary.

Dan took Brittany off guard by telling her how much he loved her and how much she meant to him. Wondering what had inspired all the sweetness, Brittany hugged Dan and asked him if he wanted to kneel down and say some prayers.

Dan did, but he needed to kneel down and do something else first: He pulled the ring from his rosary pouch, got down on one knee and proposed.

Brittany was so overcome that her new fiancé he had to ask, "Do you want the ring?"

He slid it onto her finger, and they thanked Our Lord and the Blessed Mother with a rosary together. They concluded the night with a celebratory dinner with her family.

It was easy to select a wedding date: Easter 2012. They chose the second Sunday of the celebratory spring season. What a perfect way to end a long-distance relationship and enter into the sacrament of marriage!

"We are so excited," Dan told CatholicMatch in 2011. "God is good!"

Read more tales of courtship and romance at CatholicMatch. com/blog/category/success-stories.

The
Catholic Playbooks

Guiding single Catholics through every juncture, step by step.

Don't miss the upcoming titles
in our playbook series, delivering
practical advice and spiritual wisdom:

> Healing From Divorce
> Online Dating
> Discerning A Vocation
> Dating & Relationships
> Being A Single Parent

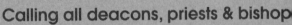